# PRESSED FLOWER
# PICTURES

13″ × 17″. The line of the picture is guided for us by a dark stalk of Clematis Montana. The leaves are the grey undersides of Raspberry; and one slightly folded little Senecio leaf contrasts with the grey. The 'Rose buds' are Senecio buds. The circle of flower petals are from the floribunda Rose Iceberg, stuck down *only* at the very inner tip of the petal. Welsh Poppy stamens make a suitable centre.

# PRESSED FLOWER PICTURES

## A VICTORIAN ART REVIVED

PAMELA McDOWALL

LUTTERWORTH PRESS · GUILDFORD & LONDON

*First Published 1969*
*Second Impression 1970*
*Third Impression 1970*
*Fourth Impression 1972*
*Fifth Impression 1974*
*First Paperback Edition 1975*
*Second Paperback Edition 1978*

## ACKNOWLEDGEMENTS

The Author wishes to acknowledge the help given by the following in the preparation of her book: Mr. and Mrs. J. D. Livingston Booth and Mr. and Mrs. Peter Williams, for permission to include pictures which are their property; Miss Jean Mauldon of the Reference Library, Tunbridge Wells, for her very kind help with technical points; Mr. Francis Drewe, who lent the seaweed pictures; Mr. Stanley Hobbs, for invaluable help; David Lawton and Percival Stickells, Camden Studios, Tunbridge Wells, for their photography; "Books and Prints", Mount Pleasant, Tunbridge Wells, for framing and backing the pictures; W. J. Walter, 7 High Street, Tunbridge Wells, for mounting board; Secretarial Services of Tunbridge Wells, for typing the manuscript; and finally, but not least, all the many friends and acquaintances, who have contributed to her collection of flowers.

Plates 4 and 15 have appeared in *House and Garden*; plates 17 and 24b and c have appeared in *Woman's Own*. The Author's photograph on the book jacket is reproduced by permission of the *Kent Messenger*.

Dosia Craig's picture appears in *A Handbook of Crafts*, by Griselda Leslie, published by Hulton Press in 1960.

**ISBN 0 7188 1654 4**

COPYRIGHT © 1969 BY PAMELA McDOWALL

PRINTED AND BOUND IN HONG KONG

# Contents

Lovely satin-like fronds of seaweed, the mature state of Ulva Linza.

# *Introduction*

IF YOU LOVE flowers as much as I do, both the wild and herbaceous flowers can be yours to look at on the walls in your house all the year round, preserved by the simple process of pressing and making pictures, table mats and door finger plates with your pressed flower collection.

It could be called a Victorian Art or Pastime Revived, for in the 1850s not only were flowers pressed by the demure Victorian Miss, but pictures too were made, with feathers delicately arranged into the shapes of flowers and leaves.

Even hair, tresses collected by the inconsolable and bereaved, was intertwined and woven in designs for pictures, framed in pear or cherry wood. Some hair was concealed into the cameo brooch, worn at a time of mourning, or in happier circumstances given by the loved one to his or her 'intended' as a Valentine.

Seaweed did not escape the hands of the nimble fingered. Ladies, not clad in bikinis or Bermuda shorts, but in long trailing gowns of taffeta and summer silks, lifted a few daring inches off the sands, traipsed up and down the beaches at low tide, searching amongst the pools and collecting some of the many seaweeds in buckets. They would then return home to lay their choices on blotting paper to press in books and later, when it had dried sufficiently, compose a picture entirely of dried pressed seaweed. These Victorian enthusiasts were guided by a book popular at the time, written by The Rev. Lansborough in 1849, *A Popular History of British Seaweeds.*

These seaweed pictures (the forerunners of the pressed flowers) survive today in museums and in scrap albums of our great-great-grandmothers, but they are scarce and hard to find. Their lacey fronds, some faded to shades of sepia, deep brown, maroon or crimson, pressed out exactly like a silken ribbon. The large detached seaweeds

Seaweed pressed in the 1850s: at the top, C. Brachiatum, which is maroon; in the middle, Laminaria Saccharina, pale green; and Griffithsia Secundiflora, crimson.

were found at high water, where rough seas had cast them up from the depths of the sea, and in the rock-pools grew the fine delicate seaweeds, which when gently pressed and dried looked like line drawings in crimson or brown ink. After collecting, the seaweed was first rinsed several times in salt water through muslin to rid it of sand. Fresh water was not used, for the weed decomposed quickly. It was then laid on perforated zinc to drain. After at least five or six rinsings the seaweed was at last put to rest on paper or blotting paper, and a brush was used to move and arrange the delicate fronds into attractive shapes, as I do nowadays.

Three or four layers of blotting paper were placed over the fronds in the drying process (whereas with flower pressing, only one is needed), and were renewed every 12–15 hours until completely dry.

I was interested to learn that for sticking the seaweed down on the paper the skin off boiled milk was used, and the paper was sponged down first with this simple adhesive.

The thicker, coarser seaweed seen in seaweed pictures was treated differently from the pool varieties. It was boiled for 20 minutes to remove the salt, and rinsed again in fresh water, and then pressed. The dainty sea-pool varieties are always red in colour and almost transparent, whereas those found in fresh water pools are of the greener colours. These were arranged on the background of Victorian pictures to represent distant hills in a landscape, and the coarser seaweed was used in the foreground to represent hedges and trees. At the end of a seaside holiday many a coachman must have groaned as he lifted the various boxes filled with seashells, for these were now to be glued on to the surround of each humble seaweed picture, and a caption beneath read, "Call us not weeds—we are flowers of the sea".

Personally, their lovely cherry or pearwood picture frames most catch my eye. In those days they could be bought for as little as a shilling.

Never, surely, was there a time in history when so many Victorian human squirrels were at work so painstakingly with so many different forms of materials for making pictures. 'Flower' pictures composed of feathers; landscape pictures in sands of different colours. Pictures of castles made entirely of cork. *Collage* in silks, felts, satins, left-overs from the ragbag of the family dressmaker. Nothing—but nothing in

8

those days was ever wasted. In the same way, in this Elizabethan age, no flowering weed is ever wasted in my garden; all are cherished and placed on the walls of my home in Flower Pictures.

In the 1830–50s, the craze was for buying packets of stamped-out tinsels. Drawings of actors, or Roman soldiers, in dramatic stances were sold to be ornamented with suitable stuck-on shapes in these various glinting coloured tinsels. The humble seaweed followed—and then pressed flowers! I was happy to see Dosia Craig had, in a Victorian pressed flower arrangement, used my favourite stalks and leaves, Clematis Montana and the Japanese Maple, Fern and Ivy. If the Victorians were incurable collectors, so then am I! I collect flowers, leaves and grasses and in this book hope to show you how this is done— for Pressed Flower Pictures.

# I

## *Why Not Try?*

ONE NOT ONLY collects flowers—but friends!

Staying in an hotel in Cornwall, I was considered a little "odd" as I set forth with a basket to walk slowly along the high-banked lanes, returning in the evening's sun with a positive convoy of butterflies which escorted me into the hotel lounge, after the scent of the honey-laden Clovers and Honeysuckle. Soon, curiosity in the other guests broke down reserve, and hardly a meal went by when I did not find a flower left on my table in the dining-room, with a note by the giver as to where it could be found should I decide it was a suitable "presser"! I made many friends this way, and some even came on wild flower walks with me. At home I keep a jam jar filled with water on the door step, just in case a friend has called when I am out, and the welcome gift need not be left to wilt.

One couple in my road have been very kind in supplying me throughout the summer with a particularly attractive species of Honeysuckle, Lonicera Halliana. My neighbours, on their return from exercising their beagle, are asked anxiously, "Did you find me a nice dark crimson Blackberry leaf or an interesting autumn leaf?" Their son, John, a Scout, returned from his holiday with a fistful of Heather from the New Forest, and this you, the reader, can see in the door finger plate design in plate 23b.

Once, fearing I would lose some Lady's Bedstraw growing in a bank of a narrow Sussex lane, I sent my Boy Scout to jump out of the car and overtake—oh! horror! the hedge-cutting machine men, who were tidying up, no doubt on Council's orders, the lovely hunting ground for Flower Power enthusiasts! He leapt out and dashed on ahead of the machine, while I crept along in low gear, hoping my "one good deed a day" lad could grab a few stems of the Lady's Bedstraw. He excelled himself! He threw himself into the exercise and ditch with enthusiasm and was in time to grab, not a handful—but one enormous armful! My two little jam jars of water to put the flowers in were totally inadequate, but the deed was accomplished, and we returned triumphant; and while my Scout licked his ice-cream reward I spent one hour of my lunch time pressing the Lady's Bedstraw before it wilted! It dries out a black colour and is very dainty.

Two friends supplied me with the dark blue Jackmanii (for contrast in tone, use the underside—it has a more interesting line running through the petal). One friend drove 18 miles to bring me some of her precious blooms. On such occasions one must see one has a good supply of blotting paper. It's best to buy a quire at a time. Blotting paper can be re-used providing it is dried off (from its previous pressing) in the airing cupboard.

No flowering weed is ever wasted in my garden. If you have no garden, take a walk into the many parks or playgrounds in autumn for the leaves of trees, and grasses, which make very decorative designs without the embellishment of flowers, or even colours other than the beiges, dark browns and crimsons. Consider and arrange a holiday where you can ramble over hills or scramble over the moorlands and glens where the lovely Saxifrages, marsh Buttercups and Heather abound. But do not pick the Scottish bluebell, the Harebell; the colour does not keep at all, so let it be.

A bus ride will surely find you a grassy verge where so many wild flowers offer scope for a pressed flower picture. One glorious sunny day, blue sky a backcloth to the rolling white cotton-wool clouds, found me climbing a winding "twitten" (pathway for sheep) to the top of Chanctonbury Hill. Puffed, tired, but happy, I lay down in the grass after reaching the top, and there, within an arm's stretch, I counted fourteen different varieties of grasses. All are cherished and placed on the walls of my home in these pressed flower pictures. Each flower, grass or leaf is a memory carried home from many parts of the country.

It is a good idea to plant your garden to suit your choice of good "pressers". Use the hedgerows, and walks over the fields and along lanes where there is a whole wealth of grasses and weeds to be be found, Cow Parsley, Goose grass (which is sticky and difficult to disentangle from one's clothes!), the dainty crimson leaves of Herb Robert (or Wild Geranium). The patron saint of Germany was named after this little wild flower, for it was reputed to have cured the plague in the 14th century. Picked in August on a sunny bank where the warmth has turned its leaves crimson, it resembles brown lace when pressed; Lady's Bedstraw—these are but a few of the many wild flowers possible to use for pressing.

I keep a special section of silver leaved plants in a well-drained, sunny part of the garden, for these silver-leaved plants show up well on a black background, and in a rather dull, drab part of the garden. The silver underside part of the Raspberry leaves can be usefully found in the kitchen garden.

The herbaceous border supports the invaluable Delphinium, and many others which will be mentioned in a list later. In the autumn months you can compose a picture entirely of leaves (see plate 12). Autumn brings continued activity to the collector just when you think the collecting is over and a rest is in sight! But no! There are so many lovely tones to be found in the autumn leaves, from the vermilion of the various Prunus, to the crimsons of the Cherry Prunus, browns of the Beech and Oak, and the lovely dark crimson of the Blackberry leaf.

During early summer, pick a number of leaves, Aspen and Poplar leaves. They are silver one side and black on the other.

The very early young Oak leaves which in April and May are tiny and crimson or pink dry out an almost transparent deep brown. Maple, too, when picked very young dries out a transparent pale green or yellow. In summer pick the dark crimson leaves of the various Japanese Maples. For sheer delight in shape, the varying serration of leaves is the thing which "makes" a picture rather than bright colour.

The very young leaves too, of the Ash tree saplings. These dry out black. Visit the tree every two weeks or so until you can pick two identical young leaves at the top of the new sapling's growth. These are most useful for the finishing off of the centre bases or focal point of your picture (see page 59). For town dwellers, as I am, there is an abundance of the lovely Prunus leaves in autumn. After the first cold nights set in for winter, a liberal selection can be found in the parks or

The leaves are Senecio, Cineraria Maritima Diamond. The large centre flowers are made from Iceberg Rose petals. Mimosa, Eggs and Bacon, Clover, Honeysuckle, Cow Parsley, Buttercups, and lawn Daisies are the other flowers. The grasses are Mousetail and Trembling. (I saw the Trembling grass in the headlights of my car after a bonfire party, growing on a bank in my host's drive.)

on the paths, and on my way home from shopping these are carefully gathered up, and the most attractive ones in shape and colour are put in a plastic bag on top of the groceries and taken home to press! There are many grasses too, to be found all summer growing along the grass verges, but in my garden the rubbish bonfire plot and tiny "orchard" (of one apple tree) is a paradise for Nipplewort, Goose grass and Ground Elder! Ground Elder despised by all, perhaps, except by flower pressers, for it has an uncontrollable desire to take over the garden. It is by me allowed to grow and "wax strong" in the orchard until it is in full flower! Its lovely little dainty white umbel of florets is very useful arranged on a black background.

In and around the more shady and damp parts of the garden, there is another useful leaf suitable for pressing, and that is the fern. They can be picked in spring and summer (see list on page 20).

All grasses are "safe", but aim for the daintiest. Other leaves, for some reason, especially the green ones, turn only to the dry colours, as in hay, but the leaves of Ash, Honeysuckle and Montana dry a welcome black and are very useful in a design.

Don't pick every flower you see in sight. It is not only wasteful to the countryside but wastes your time, and all the many quires of blotting paper that are needed to press them in.

Some imagine it is difficult to make these pictures. It isn't. It cannot be. I always say, "Any fool can do it—if I can, so can *you*!"

Remember the first effort in your Kindergarten age? What fun it all was, and the results were better if you could forget you had pressed the flower and so give it a chance to dry undisturbed. The PRIME RULE for a successful pressing is DO NOT LOOK AT your flowers for at least 6 to 8 weeks.

So why not try? Do not approach it with even one thought of failure! It is so easy providing the flower is one suggested, and tested, in this book.

All this can be fitted in at odd moments of the day. It's the thinking of the future pleasure it will bring that makes the present less of an effort.


## COLOUR

Colour is an important item even if the overall tones are predominantly cream, yellow, brown and beige (and the greys of certain leaves). These are more in harmony with the colour of the furniture than the more brilliant colours, and are more restful. It is important that the pressed flower picture is hung on a north wall and NOT in direct sunlight, otherwise early fading will result. Also, the room should not be damp.

The best for keeping their colours are the yellows and the orange and the one blue—and that is the blue of the Delphinium. For example the inviting blues of Forget-me-not, Campanulas and Cornflowers one might think kept their colour, but in fact they do not.

All Rose petals, whatever their original colour, turn cream, for example the white floribunda Iceberg, the larger Peace rose, and another floribunda, Masquerade. But if the rose petals are a deep red, they dry out deep brown. These colours blend well with, say, the orange of Montbretia, which keeps its colour well and can also be dried in its upright form for a vase decoration—under the mattress! Most yellow flowers keep their colours for about three years, but the Anthemis daisy (of which there are two varieties, the lemon yellow and the deeper chrome yellow) last the best of all the yellows. Up to ten years and so does Limnanthese or Poached Egg plant, greatly loved by bees.

Grey leaves remain grey, which is a comfort to know, when placed on either a cream or black background, and give a most delicate balance with the creams and deep browns of various other leaves.

Allow for slight fading when choosing the flowers for the design. Bear in mind that the little yellow Celandine will fade to white in a year, so do not put it in a design with a cream or white background. It comes into its own, however, placed on the maroon coloured autumn leaf of the Blackberry, or on a black background to spring flowers. That all flowers I mention do not keep their original strong colour is, to me, no matter. It is more important to get a TONE balance of creams, dark browns, and silver into a picture, and the "swing" of stalks and leaves to carry the design is more important still.

## IDEAS

An ideal way in which to combine pleasure with usefulness—and the hobby is suitable for children—is by making flower pictures as Christmas, birthday or wedding presents. Perhaps incorporate into the design flowers or leaves which your friends had contributed from their

15

24″ × 34″. This was one of my earlier pictures, but already simplicity is coming into the design. Clematis Montana stalk, Japanese Maple leaves, Clematis Jackmanii, and Cow Parsley; a few Hydrangea florets, Maidenhair fern (bought at a florist's), and a pretty fluffy weed which a friend brought back from a holiday in Austria. I struggled for days over this design. It would not come right, and it was not till I accidentally tripped and knocked the board with my foot that the design was "knocked into shape". The picture can be hung horizontally or perpendicularly.

garden to your pressing collection earlier on in the year? Encourage the children especially to choose their flowers carefully and discriminately. Collecting makes a dull walk into an exciting exploration and adventure, and a reason for the walk—to pick a few Daisies, Buttercups, Cow Parsley and ferns and make a picture in the autumn months. Wrap a little moist moss around the stems to keep the flowers fresh in hot little hands until home is reached. The children could start with a simple design for a door finger plate for their bedroom doors, or a table mat to present to grandparents at Christmas time.

Door finger plates and table mats of pressed flowers are eagerly bought up at bazaars, and once it gets around where they were made, watch out! You may be inundated with orders. So a word of advice. Keep back a few small mats or finger plates in reserve, to give you time to 'draw breath', for there is nothing more destroying to a hobby than to turn it into a grind! Nothing spoils a design more than tension, or pressure to work to a given time.

Choose a holiday, be it overseas or on home ground, where, when you have explored the local architectural antiquities, you may seek out the wild flowers, press them as you go along, put them between blotting paper in a book and tie it tight with string, and do as I once did in an hotel on holiday.

Determined not to miss adding some especially choice flowers I had found to my collection, the problem was, where was the heavy weight to be found to place *on* the pressing book? It was solved by putting the book under the leg of the bed! For the first night I slept "crooked", but by the second night another book of freshly gathered Clovers and grasses under the other leg had made things equal. By the time my stay was over, the room was scented like the hayfield it nearly became, and the long-suffering maid (when she knew of my hobby) left the flowers pressing happily alone!

It is a lovely, rewarding way to be reminded of a happy holiday, with your "souvenirs" in frames on your walls, doors or tables! When skies were overcast, the guests in the hotel missed their sun-bathing on the sands, and were almost at a loss for what to do with themselves, while I was as happy as a country cricket exploring the lonely lanes and moorland for special flowers. To see the flowers which once grew around them at a picnic peeping out from a table mat beneath a plate can, while the hostess at the dinner party goes to bring in the next course, give the guests plenty to gaze upon and talk about!

Then, if you become more proficient in the art of pressing flowers, and you have made a sufficient number of pictures, table mats and finger plates, offer your services for a small fee to the secretary of any local Women's Institute or Friendship Guild in the town or villages around you, and give a talk and demonstration on your hobby. If you do not wish to accept a fee, then ask if you may pass round the hat for a charity, in a special collecting tin provided by the charity you choose. It is a nice way of collecting for a good cause.

The next step after giving talks can be an exhibition of your pictures in a local hall provided in most towns for just this purpose, and can be very rewarding, if it is known you wish to sell the pictures.

An idea, too, could be to make a Valentine card. Construct it out of black or red paper. Stick frilled lace round the "heart" of a Rose (for the petals of a Rose are heart-shaped). It might not be a red "heart", because a Rose petal fades to brown or fawn in a year, but a deep red Rose petal may, if you are lucky, last until February 14th if it is not exposed at all to daylight until near that date. Circle the "heart" with frilly lace, cut from the outer edges of a paper doyley, and your card will then very much resemble the lovely Victorian paper-laced Valentines of the 1860s. Daisies and Buttercups would be pretty, their stems curved to encircle the "heart", and the whole picture need only be covered with cellophane stretched tightly over it all, and stuck down behind the paper or cardboard backing.

Beneath the flowers could be the words:

"I'm a little prairie flower,
Growing wilder every hour.
No one's going to cultivate me
Unless of course—it could be
THEE."

# 2

## A Choice of Flowers and Foliage

*Flowers*
Anthemis
Astrantia (or Hattie's Pincushion)
Auricula
Bog Sandwort
Broom
Buttercup
Buttercup, Marsh
Celandine
Clematis Jackmanii, Nelly Moser, President, Mme Edward André, Florida Bicolor
Clover
Coreopsis
Cosmos
Cow Parsley
Daffodil (big all yellow trumpet variety)
Daisy (lawn Daisy only)
Delphinium
Eggs and Bacon (Bird's-foot Trefoil)
Golden Rod
Goose grass
Ground Elder
Heather
Heuchera Sanguinea
Honeysuckle
Hydrangea
Laburnum
Lady's Bedstraw

19

Limnanthese (Poached Egg plant)
Marigold
Mimosa (3 varieties)
Mimulus
Montbretia
Pansy (yellow and black only) and Wild
Poppy: Iceland (also red, yellow and orange Welsh and Shirley)
Primula and Polyanthus
Rose petals
Saxifrage
Statice
Sutton's Sunshine Flower (*Venidio Arctotis*)
Tobacco plant
Tulip
Vetch

*Grasses*
Barley, Wild
Barren Brome
Mousetail
Pond grass
Trembling grass

*Ferns*
Hard Fern and Holly Fern
Common Polypody and Limestone Polypody
Maidenhair Spleenwort
Mountain Buckler Fern

*Leaves*
Aspen (silver)
Ash
Beech
Blackberry
Centaurea Gymnocarpa (grey)
Cinerarea Maritima Diamond (grey)

Clematis Montana
Earth Nut (or Pig Nut)
Echinops or Globe Thistle
Hellibore
Herb Robert (Wild Geranium)
Honeysuckle
Honesty (very young seed pods)
Ivy
Japanese Maple
Maple
Oak
Poplar
Prunus
Raspberry (underside only)
Senecio
Vetch
Whitebeam

## Stalks
Suitable also as a substitute for other less curvey, resilient stalks.
Anthemis
Buttercups
Clover
Montana
Primrose

## Centres
Dried, pressed Marigold or Poppy centres can be used (if the petals
have fallen off) for, say, the centre of a Rose. So can the white Astrantai,
Hattie's Pincushion.


### ANTHEMIS
This yellow herbaceous Daisy (rather like the Pyrethrum daisy which I
have not as yet tried) is ideal and the best flower of all for colour
retention (ten years to date!). There are two colour varieties, a pale

yellow and a deeper, more chrome colour. The white one is Anthemis Montana shown in plate 5. Pick the flower at the correct time, which is on about its third day of opening in July. Press its stems separately, preferably in a curve. Success lies in not waiting until all its numerous tiny florets in the middle are forming too fully, for they make a very undesirable lump, and this is very difficult to flatten in drying. Press the thumb down very hard and firmly on its middle and close the book quickly. Anthemis needs the heaviest weight of all the flowers.

### ASTRANTIA OR HATTIE'S PINCUSHION

This most welcome, star-like flower can be of either a white or a rose pink variety. Its reverse side is as pretty as its front, the calyxes being a greeny pink colour. You can see an example of this in plate 14 on the left-hand side (at 10 o'clock), showing both the front of the flower and the back. It can also be placed in the centre of rose petals to resemble a white star, as Mrs. Ginger has done (see page 69).

### AURICULA

This is of the Primula family. Pick the startling deep mauve and white or cream sort only. Pull the flowers off their stalks, and leaving the stamens and calyx behind, press your thumb firmly on the flower and roll the book's pages over quickly to get them without a bent or curled petal. Place the flower head right up close to the binding of the book. This goes for all flower heads.

### BOG SANDWORT

This is found in Teesdale, Scotland; and it would be a suitable plant to press. It is very dainty, and especially lends itself to design because of its slim, pencil-like stalks. I cannot emphasise too much the importance of stalks, they take the place of the drawn line in a pen and ink sketch.

### BROOM

Broom dries out a startling and surprising black or very dark brown, and can be worked into a design of beiges and yellows.

## BUTTERCUP

These are the easiest to press and the colour lasts about three or four years. The field Buttercup has more dainty stalks and leaves than its cousin the bulbous Buttercup, which has a deeper, stronger yellow, and you can superimpose the daintier stalk of the one on to the better, bigger flower of the other. Press flower and stalks all in one. I discovered that the Buttercups in Cornwall were particularly large, some with as many as seven petals instead of the more normal five in Kent and Sussex! I brought home in an old empty cornflake carton the most precious souvenir of my holiday, a root of this rather lush Buttercup. It now grows in my own little garden, and though it is a weed it is tended and cultivated as if it were from a nursery garden! I hope it will multiply.

## BUTTERCUP, MARSH

This is very pretty and dainty, but, like its bigger cousin of the Ranunculus family, it loses its colour in about three years. This fading will not really spoil the picture, if the Buttercup is placed on a black background.

## CELANDINE

These grow in profusion in a country lane, in a moist soil, yet sunny enough to keep the petals open. I gathered them with my Boy Scout neighbour as his good deed for the day; you must work fast with Celandines, as they close up so quickly when picked. Together we picked a book full, pressed there and then in the car, page by page between blotting paper before they rapidly closed in the shade. Celandines look lovely on a black background or on a dark leaf, for, remember, Celandines turn white after a year. Pick them in full sun at midday.

## CLEMATIS

My next favourite as a flower for a design (but not for its original pinky-mauve colour) is the Clematis Nelly Moser. Use the petals reverse side up. This flower, while it is still in its pressing stage, gradually turns a gentle burnt sienna colour with a most attractive darker line down the middle of each petal, exactly the same colouring as the

23

stripe on a donkey's back. Press each petal separately, as this Clematis has a very thick centre. Do not use the lumpy centre at all.

Nelly Moser is ideal for the start of a large design. Place several slightly off-centre, work round them, and then outwards.

Clematis Jackmanii is a very striking and welcome dark black-blue colour. Its dark tone can be needed to set off the lighter petals of say the Celandine, lawn Daisy or Mimosa. Use for a stalk the twisting twine and swirl of the Montana's "twiggle". New growths appear in early summer and autumn, and with them you can give the design a lovely swinging movement. Alternate the petals of the Jackmanii, the dark top side and then the reverse side uppermost, to get a paler tone (as shown in plate 3, a large design with Echinops silver leaves and large Peace Rose petals to contrast with the small Iceberg Rose petals). Clematis Madame Edward André (red) dries out maroon coloured, like a Blackberry leaf in autumn. See plate 10.

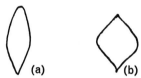

Once, being short of the more arrow (a) shape petals of Nelly Moser, I cut the dark blue (b) spade-shape petals of Jackmanii into the long pointed shape I needed.

## CLOVER

Clover is a nice "rounded" flower to press. Not spectacular perhaps in its humble beige colouring, but valuable for its shape, and especially useful if its stalk can be pressed with a nice curve. Pick only the white variety. This flower needs extra weight in pressing, like the Anthemis, Marigold and Mimosa. Clover is one of the flowers I cheat with, to emphasise its circular sepal arrangement. When it is pressed and dried, apply a very little white poster paint to the circular and interesting "whirl" effect it has. It makes all the difference to highlight, as it were, its circle in the middle of the florets. The white clover is suitable for a black or cream background design.

## COREOPSIS

Use the petals only. They have a lovely maroon colour at the inside centre of the yellow petal, and the colour keeps well.

COSMOS

There are a number of useful colours ranging from pale mauve to the deeper mauve and the deep rose pink. These keep their colour for quite six or seven years and the petals can be pressed singly or the flower in its entirety (not the stalks). To get a deeper tone, place (when dried) one on top of the other. (Do this also with the Welsh and Iceland Poppies and Marigolds.)

COW PARSLEY

For sheer daintiness pick the common Cow Parsley, this hedgerow and roadside flower. Do not pick the stalks or leaves, and here again touch up the tiny white florets very slightly with white poster paint as they become a little fawn coloured with the years. Cow Parsley looks lovely dotted about on a black background.

DAFFODIL (Yellow, large trumpet variety)

Pick these in spring, or as early as you like at a florist's. Do not press the flower as a whole, but nip off the green seedbox and stalk and slice the trumpet in half, as shown in the illustrations on page 46, leaving the three petals on either side and half its trumpet to press. Arrange to dry, and press no more than two to a page in the pressing book. They look well on a black or cream-coloured background.

DAISY (lawn Daisy)

One of my favourites! Pick it stalk and all in full midday sun; and when the designing stage arrives, place either way up on the board. The dark green calyx is as attractive as their little yellow "middles", and very pretty, especially if the petals are edged underneath at the tips with crimson. This often happens if the cultivated Bachelor Button daisy happens to have been growing in the vicinity. When pressed and quite dry, you may paint the petals with white poster paint.

DELPHINIUM

No other flower, in my experience of trial and error, will keep its blue colour for so long except its nearest relation, the Larkspur. My Delphinium blue has lasted in a table mat so far for ten years. I have some

FLEURS DE JÉRUSALEM

POSÉES SUR LE SAINT SÉPULCRE

FLEURS DE    BÉTHLÉHEM

POSÉES SUR LE SAINT SÉPULCRE

Pressed flowers from the Holy Land, dated 1883: taken from a Victorian scrap album.

These pressed flowers from Jaffa were sent in 1889. The Delphiniums are still blue.

very old pressed flowers from the Holy Land found in an 1880 scrap-album (see above). Among the flowers below the designs (depicting the Crucifixion, and Mary at the Holy Sepulchre) are some Larkspurs or Delphiniums. I can just see the pale blue on the petals. The date on the back of one is 1883, and on the other 1889, from Jaffa, which sends a Christmas greeting to England in Arabic.

Admittedly they have been kept in a closed book and away from the strong sunlight, but eighty years is proof that the Delphinium keeps its colour. This is one of the flowers (like the Marigold) which take a little

26

longer to dry out. With Delphiniums only, it helps to dismantle each petal and dry them separately, twenty or so petals to a page. Whether or not you need do this depends on whether it is a good summer. If it is not, the very depth and number of petals in a floret may make it dry out with a slight spotting of mould.

It is a good idea to press some separately, some in their entirety (not the stalks), buds and all, as well as some dismantled petal by petal. This is not as laborious as it sounds! You must reassemble them later in the year when you come to the designing, but it is very well worth while, as each separate petal dries perfectly. One can by this method make more "Delphiniums", and perhaps a "mock" Periwinkle, as shown in one of the door-finger plate designs in plate 23b.

### EGGS AND BACON (Bird's Foot Trefoil)

Another yellow flower, but this dries out sometimes to a cream, sometimes to a strange pale green; but it is delicate and curvey and welcome.

### GOLDEN ROD

Press each little flower stalk separately.

### GOOSE GRASS AND LADY'S BEDSTRAW

These are two interesting grass-type wild flowers, for foliage and stalks only. The flowers are too small and insignificant. Both these weeds make good dark flowing lines for the corners of a picture. Goose grass is sticky and clinging owing to its serrated covering on the leaves and stalks. Lady's Bedstraw is lovely, like very fine, dainty black lace.

### GROUND ELDER

This I've mentioned earlier, and its distant cousin Cow Parsley. It is surely the gardeners' most unloved weed-plant, because it creeps into a garden in a most insidious way, and it is soon among their most cherished herbaceous plants if they do not keep a very vigilant eye on its bright green leaf! This otherwise unloved weed comes into its own, however, with its umbrella-like span of white flowers, which, after pressing, can be used for door finger plate designs. They are also very striking and dainty placed on a black background. This floret too can be touched up with white poster paint when you make your design.

HEATHER

Though it has hard stalks, enough can be removed to leave the little purple flower which keeps its colour well.

HEUCHERA SANGUINEA

This is like a small coral pink Saxifrage or London Pride, and is a great favourite of mine. It is very dainty, and its long slender stem looks lovely among grey leaves, or the leaves of the dark Cherry Prunus.

HONEYSUCKLE

This is almost the most decorative and most used dried pressed flower in my collection. To press, pick off every floret, including the tiny un-opened buds and semi-open flowers, and then reassemble all the florets when dried exactly as they once grew as the hedgerow variety.

Honeysuckle Lonicera Halliana, however, is the loveliest variety of all. The long slender trumpets grow off singly, in pairs, up the stalk, and not all in the one combined umbel at the top (like the hedgerow variety), but when dried I turn it into the common hedgerow variety. The beige colour will remain, and with a butterfly hovering near it (as shown in the small table mat photographs, plates 21b and c), they complete the picture.

Honeysuckle is a MUST! Most countryside hedges have some.

HYDRANGEA

These are not as complicated as they seem. Each floret is nipped off and pressed separately thirty or forty to a page. Most dry out to a beige or green, and they are useful for scattering on a light-toned background. Some florets when picked green (the tiny ones in the centre) look well in an orange, yellow and brown design, which I have used in the large picture in plate 18.

28

I once made a set of a dozen table mats, each mat entirely made up of Hydrangea florets, assembled into the one, original shape. Place the paler petals at the top of the circle and the darker, crimson ones at the circle's base. This gives a shading effect, and makes the design look more rounded. The colours last for about three years.

### LABURNUM

Laburnum means Forsaken in the language of flowers, but it is not by me! It does not hold its pretty lemon yellow at all but turns cream. I include it, like the Broom, for its interesting shape alone.

### LADY'S BEDSTRAW AND WOODRUFF

Both dry out black like the Goose grass, black, lacy and dainty. They grow in banks and ditches. The Woodruff prefers shadier places, and both flower in June.

### LIMNANTHESE OR POACHED EGG PLANT

Grown for bordering round the flower beds and for bees' pasture. This is another yellow which keeps its colour one of the longest, and it is most effective on a black background in a small table mat (as shown on page 64). Nip off the stalks before pressing.

### MARIGOLD

These keep their orange colour for about a year only. After that they become a lovely pale beige. When dry, place two upon each other, and this extra flower will prove rewarding in later years. The marigold must be picked on a very dry, sunny day. It takes many weeks to dry out really well. These are the only flowers I look at (as well as the *entire* floret of the Delphinium) after about three weeks of pressing, and I change their blotting paper to a new dry sheet, if the flower is dry enough to move without disturbing the petals. The centres are most useful for using as "middles" to superimposed flowers: for example, Statice can be made to "grow" from a discarded Marigold middle.

## MIMOSA

There are three varieties, and being yellow they keep their colour quite well. It is a lovely flower subject and lends itself to many designs, especially if it can be persuaded to be curvaceous when placed in the books to dry. Take off each little frond from the main thicker stem. Bend the little stem as much as is possible. I prefer the non-fluffy variety. These curved fronds of little blobs of yellow are most attractive, placed, say, on a dark crimson Blackberry leaf. Mimosa shows up well with the darker tones, placed on the Jackmanii's dark blue petals, or on the dark maroon colour of the Cherry Prunus leaves, as in plate 11a. Mimosa arranged in a little fan-like design looks quite lovely in a group of spring flowers arranged on a black background.

Mimosa needs a very heavy weight on the books when drying. Do not use the Mimosa leaves, except the very pointed thin-leaved variety.

## MIMULUS

Both the spotted red and yellow, and brown and yellow, Mimulus press very well and make an interesting splash of colour. The red Mimulus presses out to a deep brown. Press the flower only. It is a pondside plant and likes moist soil.

## MONTBRETIA

Montbretia flowers and buds keep their colour very well. Take off the *open* flowers and press them separately. Also press the small unopened fronds of buds (see plate 14). You can also preserve Montbretia for an upright flower display. Just place them under your mattress in bed and forget about them for about four weeks.

## NIPPLEWORT

This is a must. Pick and press it when it is in early bud and in seed, but shake the seeds out first.

## PANSY

The best ones for retaining their colour are the yellow and black-faced Pansies *only*.

## PANSY, WILD

This little flower is sometimes known as "Jump-up-and-kiss-me", or "Jack in the Hedge", or "*Pensez à moi*", Think of me. They are not very common, but they are certainly found in Scotland.

## POPPY, ICELAND

The little yellow Poppy is most delicate and lovely. Its petals turn to a most welcome pale orange (melon colour) and last about three years; therefore "strengthen" it by placing another group of petals beneath it, when you come to use it in a design. To press these Poppies, pinch out their centre "seed box" and stigma. If preferred, press the petals separately and reassemble them when dry. Take off the stalk. The flowers are very fragile, but do not be put off by the rounded and crinkly petals. Be brave! Just close the pages on them, and you will see, they will press most beautifully and look like orange satin when dry. You must almost hold your breath when arranging them on the board for the design and before sticking them in place, a heavy sigh and they will float off and away! Substitute the stalk of the Poppy with the Anthemis stalk.

## PRIMULA AND POLYANTHUS

The pondside, water-loving, red-pink Primula forms a very usefully shaped petal and dries out to a browny mauve. Both the Primula and Polyanthus can have the same treatment on pressing as the Auricula. Pick the Primula flower off the stalk, press the thumb firmly down on it and close the book quickly. Pick the red Polyanthus. It turns a deep mauvy brown. Don't pick Cowslip, it turns green!

## ROSE PETALS

For a cream and brown toned picture Rose petals are lovely to use and indispensable. They must be pressed singly, about twelve petals only to a page, else moulding will result. See the petals do not touch each other when in the drying process. Rose petals press smoothly and well; but no Rose petal keeps its colour; all turn varying shades of cream or brown. A deeper brown if the petal is of a red Rose, creamy ivory if a white Rose. For the latter, I use the floribunda Iceberg, and I use Masquerade at its varying stages of changing colours when growing. It goes from yellow to pink and then to red. The large Peace Rose petals press very well. I pick the petals separately through the summer, and remember to pick them on a sunny day and only after the dew has dried out. All these charming heart-shaped petals could be used in a Valentine design. When dried, place in a circle, one petal slightly overlapping the other, discarding any that are slightly imperfect. Do not pick the leaves.

### SAXIFRAGE

Various purple Saxifrages can be found on the cliffs of Perthshire and Angus. But Saxifrage is more easily found (the pink variety) in one's own rockery!

### STATICE

The Sea Lavender, *Limonium sinuatum*: the colours are mauve, pink, yellow, white and blue. Pull off each tiny floret, and press in a mass on one page. You can buy Statice at Christmas-time and in July at a florist's. It is fun to use the florets as a "mock" flower.

### SUTTON'S SUNSHINE FLOWER *(Venidio arctotis)*

I mention this flower with some trepidation, for it is a little temperamental, as well as needing great care when it is dry and you are removing it from its blotting paper bed. But it is a lovely bloom, like a Pyrethrum, and it receives the same treatment in firm pressing as the Anthemis. It *must* be picked in full sun, and rushed straight up into the flower pressing book, as it closes as soon as it reaches the shade. It really is magnificent when pressed, every brown petal standing out clearly. It comes in all colours of browns, bronze, orange, sepia, brick reds and yellow ochre. The choice is yours.

### TOBACCO PLANT

Rather disappointing as a "presser", but for its unusual shape, like a trumpet, the flower makes a change from the more usual petal arrangements. Nip off the flower and press by rolling the book's pages over, to see that the petals go really flat. It dries out a creamy colour.

## TULIP

I have only dried one Tulip, and that was a big red, black and yellow-petalled variety. The red faded to a shiny beige and the yellow, streaked with a deeper sepia, resembling shiney silk. An intriguing petal, and they can all be pressed separately (like the Rose and Honeysuckle) and then reassembled when dried: unusual, and with great possibilities for a cream-toned picture. I intend to try more of them in future.

## VETCH

Though their green leaves and stalks do not keep for very long in colour, their leaves are useful for their formation. They look very neat at the centre base of a design curving down either side, two identical leaves. I once spent a week hunting through my book for two leaves exactly the same in length and curve (you can see them if you turn to plate 18). They would have been more easily found had the name tag (so essential for the quick finding of a required flower, leaf or stalk) not somehow got misplaced. The flowers, especially the yellow and the blue Vetch, dry out a very pale cream.

There will be, of course, other varieties of flowers which as yet I have not got round to 'testing out', but perhaps the yellow Zinnia and yellow Dahlia might be possible "pressers", providing the petals are dismantled and dried separately—so have a go! Experiment.

*Grasses*

Keep a special book for these. An old out-of-date wall-paper pattern book can sometimes be had at a paint and wall-paper shop. This is especially useful and suitable, and can take in its huge pages the stalks of the grasses.

BARLEY, WILD

Barley can be pressed whole, and then if you need a "sparkling effect", as shown in the black background of plate 13, insert dismantled Barley whiskers between a few of the Anthemis petals.

BARREN BROME GRASS

A lovely silvery whispy grass seen on the cover and in plate 13.

TREMBLING GRASS

You can get these dainty grass stems to bend in any convenient curve, when they are needed to give "line" and direct the eye.

I cannot emphasise too often the part that the stalks of the flowers play in the balance of a picture. By stroking the stem over very firmly several times with your nail it will eventually do as you wish! When sticking the stalks just stroke a *very* little Copydex along the stalks. The outline of a flower picture is greatly "softened" by filling in the spaces with tiny grasses, and this does away with any hard outline at the edge.

*Ferns*

### HARD FERN

This can be found at an altitude of 4,000 feet in the Scottish Highlands, but I have no farther to go than to the steps and crannies of my own little shady rockery. It likes a damp and acid soil, shady ravines and banks. Its leaves have two forms (as seen in the photograph on page 48).

The barren fronds are those on the left-hand top side. They have a spreading posture, are prettier and less hard to the eye and grow nearer to the ground.

The fertile leaves, however, are more erect and have a dark brown midrib stalk. They look rather like the teeth of a comb. You can see the barren frond of this fern in several of the pictures where a curve is needed. The barren fronds are green and remain thus for some years, and they are both tougher and longer lasting than say, the bracken type of ferns. The fertile, hard-looking frond must be used sparingly. It makes a very hard striking design if carefully arranged, and not over done. Remember the saying, "It's the spaces which count!" so do not be tempted to put every flower you have ever picked into your first picture! You will regret it, and you will have the depressing business of taking out the extra flowers, leaves, and grasses, and, what is much more boring, putting them all back again into their correctly labelled pages. A most wearisome task!

### MAIDENHAIR SPLEENWORT or COMMON WALL SPLEENWORT

These like limestone and get their roots embedded into the crevices of old walls. The fronds are tiny sprays of deep green. Very dainty, and only a few inches long. I found my first in a wall in Fowey. It grows from May to October and is, like the Vetch leaves, useful for finishing off a centre base to a picture.

### COMMON POLYPODY FERN

Also to be found in the lanes of Devon and Cornwall. I discovered mine in abundance, growing in the banks of the narrow Cornish lanes,

35

at Praa Sands. You can see this fern in the left-hand corner spray of the picture on plate 14. They like to grip on to the rich deposits of leaf mould growing under the hedge banks. It is a tough fern and, I hope, will last longer than the next one.

LIMESTONE POLYPODY

This is very delicate and dainty. It is shown in the centre of the fern photograph on page 42. It goes brown, like bracken, and *might*, I fear, disintegrate, as it is so frail.

HOLLY FERN

This is *Polystichum loncliitis*. It can be found in the Lake District in Westmorland, and from Stirling to Caithness in Scotland.

*Leaves, Seed-Pods*

**ASPEN**

This tree looks lovely in a light breeze. Its silver and black leaves are continually on the "flutter". Use the silver underside uppermost on a black background. The silver poplar can be treated similarly.

**ASH**

When young, two identical dark green leaves can be seen growing out of the end of the young sapling. Visit the sapling every two or three weeks until you can find two more such identical leaves in size and curve. They dry out completely black.

**BEECH**

Pick either "on the turn" in autumn or when very very young and a tender green. They then dry out almost a transparent yellowy green.

**BLACKBERRY LEAVES**

Only pick these in late autumn when they are turning crimson, and in May and June when very tender and young, with a slight brownish look.

**CENTAUREA GYMNOCARPA**
**CINERAREA MARITIMA DIAMOND**

These two varieties are a welcome contrast and both are grey-leaved plants.

Cineraria Diamond is the smaller one, almost white on the underside and grey on top.

Centaurea Gymnocarpa is the taller, thinner leaved one. I grew mine from seeds which germinated in the record time of six days, in my own "greenhouse"—namely the airing-cupboard (with the door left open). If this method of raising seeds raises a few eyebrows, may I say that all these grey-leaved plants started life amongst my sheets and pillow cases! Within a few weeks they were able to be pricked out into roomier "lodgings", and transplanted out into boxes and kept on a bedroom window sill (the fan window always open). When the

April and May frosts were over, they were bedded out in the grey-leaved plot and showed up well in this rather dull and well drained part of the garden. But beware of snails! I dotted a number of these white-grey leaves all over the garden—anywhere and between everything as they are so useful.

### CLEMATIS MONTANA

Do not use the white flower (it will only turn fawn) but the leaves and stalks (or bind) are indispensable. Both dry out black, and the stalk (or "twiggle" as I call it) is *the* guiding line in most of my big designs. With a leaf or two placed here and there on an almost otherwise grey and "soft" toned picture, it can suddenly be brought to "life", with this graceful shape of the black leaf.

### EARTH NUT (also known as PIG NUT)

This has a dainty, lacey leaf which comes first in April, and later it flowers resembling a miniature Cow Parsley.

### ECHINOPS OR GLOBE THISTLE

A summer herbaceous plant with a round blue globe-like flower. The flowers can be dried in upright form but must be picked just as the flower is coming into bloom. They can be used for a dried vase arrangement, like Montbretia and Delphinium. I grow Echinops for its spear-like leaves. They are among the best, green on the topside, but turn it over and admire the lovely blue grey underneath side. It is a tough leaf and stands up well to a more drastic treatment than drying between sheets of blotting paper, a Quick Dry method which will be described in the technique section later in the book (page 45). Echinops, the blue Globe Thistle flower, means "hedgehog".

### HELLIBORE

The leaves can be pressed as a substitute for the leaves of the Delphinium, as they dry out a very dark strong green; but they pale slightly after three or four years. The leaf resembles a hen's foot, but with two extra claws!

**HERB ROBERT** (or Wild Geranium)

These grow on banks, in the August sun turn a browny red, and are like lace.

**HONEYSUCKLE**

It is essential to pick the leaves of the honeysuckle, whether they are placed with the honeysuckle flower or not, as they turn a very dark brown, and so can be usefully employed for "backing" behind the yellow petals of Anthemis Daisy. I have used these leaves in plate 14. The black-brown leaves have a black, star-like appearance, and set the yellow points of the petals off well.

**HONESTY**

Only use the very very young small seed pods of Honesty. They will have reached their green stage about the middle of July. (They look a bit like tadpoles to me!) Use them for finishing off a neat centre base. See page 58 and plate 18.

**IVY**

Although Ivy's dark green fades to light brown in about five years, it is useful as a base filler (see plate 24).

**JAPANESE MAPLE**

Pick these leaves at all stages and sizes throughout the spring and summer.

**MAPLE**

Maple should be picked in early spring, when the terminal leaves are just awakening, and in varying stages of opening, from crimson, pink to green. They dry out into an almost paper-thin lovely transparency.

**OAK**

Either pick the leaves when they are very young (like the Ash and Maple) when they are pinky red, and dry out a deep brown; or pick when the Oaks are in autumn leaf. Unlike flowers, the autumn leaves may be picked up in rain and pressed while damp. They are tough, and can be gently rubbed over with a nail brush to get rid of the summer's grit and grime. Turkey Oak has a lovely serrated leaf, especially useful if pressed to curve slightly.

## PRUNUS

These leaves abound on most town streets, and autumn is the time to
gather up these varying tones of vermilion, red or sandy brown leaves.
Collect them on your way home from shopping! The flowering Cherry
Prunus has a lovely dark maroon, almost black leaf, and when the tree
is pruned in late summer, the leaves which shoot out soon afterwards
come down later in a lighter shade of crimson. Pick about five or six
inches of the twig and leaves, and press in their entirety, as the twig is
very thin. (See plate 10 for a picture of these leaves, which make useful
backing for the yellow Mimosa.)

## RASPBERRY

Use the silvery grey underside of the leaf. It is one of my favourite
grey leaves.

## SENECIO GREYII

This is a shrub from which cuttings can be very easily taken. The
leaves can be used alternately, grey side up or the underside, which is
white. They look lovely on a picture with a black background, among
the yellows of Buttercup and Anthemis, Limnanthese, white lawn
Daisy, cream Rose petals and grasses. They are very satisfying to work
with. Also as the small lawn Daisy's leaf is no good for pressing or
colour-keeping, substitute a small Senecio leaf, which is similar.

## VETCH

This has already been mentioned as a useful, neat finishing off as a base.
See the Centre Bases illustration on page 59.

## WHITEBEAM

Use the underside of the Whitebeam leaf, which is a soft silver grey,
like the Raspberry.

**ANTHEMIS** and **POPPY**

Press the stalks separately from the flower heads. Keep a special book for stalks and see they are *labelled*!

**BUTTERCUPS**

All kinds, but I prefer the thinner, more dainty stalks of the field Buttercup.

**CLEMATIS MONTANA**

This has a hard stalk, so before putting into the pressing book, place it on a piece of blotting paper and another piece on top and then roll a pencil up and down it. This helps to squeeze out a little of the moisture. Don't press too hard, but it must not dry out too lumpy, otherwise, as with any one lumpy corolla, the flowers will not be pressed up flat enough against the glass when framed. Leave the stalks out of water for several hours before pressing. To avoid slight mildew appearing, just before framing take a fine paint-brush dipped in Savlon (or any mild disinfectant) and stroke it down the stalks.

**CLOVER**

When pressing, encourage them to curve; they are more useful this way than in a dead straight line, and you'll wish a thousand times (when short of a curving line) that you had taken more trouble to close the pressing book when your Clovers were in a bending shape!

Stalks are about the only part of a plant that improve by leaving them out of water for an hour, when they are in a nice relaxed and curved state for placing in their blotting paper beds!

**PRIMROSE**

Although I do not now use the flower itself the stalks are often in use with other flowers whose stalks are too unbending.

# 3

## *Technique*

### PICKING AND PRESSING

Sᴋɪʟʟ ɪs ɴᴏᴛ essential, but patience, determination, and a strong will ɴᴏᴛ to look into your pressing books for at least six weeks are ᴍᴏsᴛ important. Life becomes so "pressurised" at the height of the flower pressing season, April to September, that I myself never have time to look at my previous pages of flowers, lying, I hope, drying in their blotting paper beds until October.

**The elegant shapes of fern fronds.**

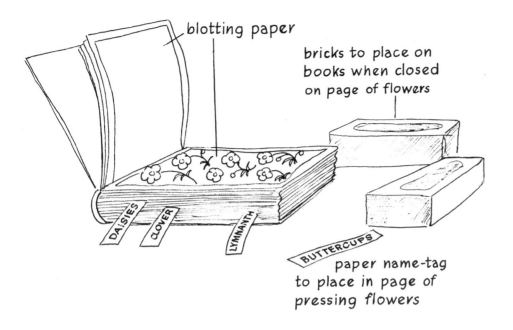

blotting paper

bricks to place on books when closed on page of flowers

DAISIES
CLOVER
LYMNANTH

BUTTERCUPS

paper name-tag to place in page of pressing flowers

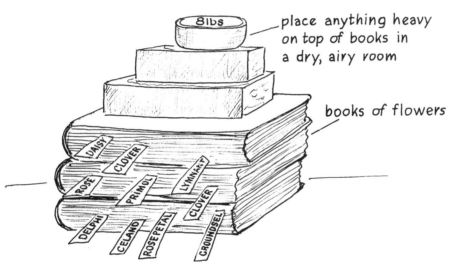

8lbs

place anything heavy on top of books in a dry, airy room

books of flowers

DAISY
CLOVER
ROSE
PRIMUL
LYMNANT
CLOVER
DELPHI
CELAND
ROSEPETAL
GROUNDSEL

*The Method*

Pick your flower, and after nipping off its stalk place it between two pieces of blotting paper in a book, the pages of which are of the thick, absorbent type, *not* of the shiny, slippery sort of paper. Weight the book very heavily with several bricks.

Pick not earlier than midday, when the bloom has had a chance to open fully and dry off the early morning dew. Some flowers, such as

43

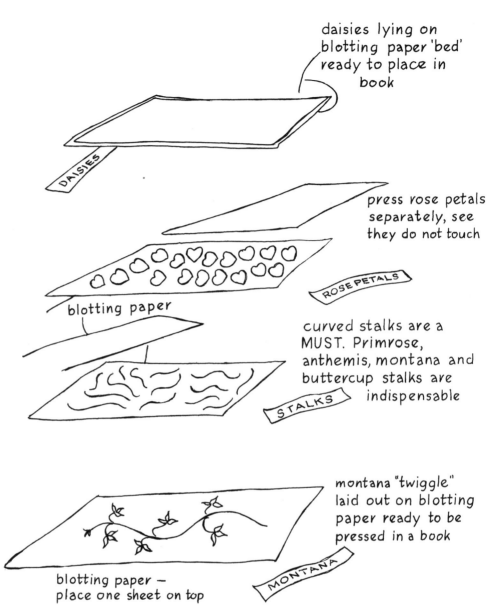

daisies lying on blotting paper 'bed' ready to place in book

DAISIES

press rose petals separately, see they do not touch

ROSE PETALS

blotting paper

curved stalks are a MUST. Primrose, anthemis, montana and buttercup stalks are indispensable

STALKS

montana "twiggle" laid out on blotting paper ready to be pressed in a book

MONTANA

blotting paper — place one sheet on top

Anthemis, lawn Daisy and Marigold, all have a habit of flinging their petals either inwards or backwards as the sun goes down.

*Never* pick after the rain. Wait a full dry day, for however fresh the flowers look after the rain, pressed damp they will only result in a lot of wasted energy, blotting paper and spotted mildewed petals.

Having picked the chosen flower, place it between the sheets of blotting paper, taking care all the petals are flat, first pressing the

44

centre corolla hard and firmly with the thumb to give it an extra start. Finally, having placed the flowers well inside and up near to the book's binding, give the pages a sort of "rolling over" on to the flower (see the Daffodil photographs, pages 46–47), so that all the petals will be rolled flat, and they stay like that when the bricks are placed on to the books.

If one flower has a very hard, thick middle, such as Clematis or Honeysuckle, take off all the petals and press them separately, and reassemble the flower when dry exactly as it grew.

When you go out collecting flowers or grasses, it is a good idea to take with you a little jam jar of water to keep them fresh as they are gathered. There is nothing more sad (and unnecessary) than to see a hot fistful of little flowers dying, never perhaps to recover before you reach the ultimate goal—home and the pressing books!

*Name Tags or Paper Slips:* These are very important to slip into your pages. Write the name of what you are pressing with various coloured felt pens in bold clear writing, yellow lettering for Buttercups, brown for Montana, Green for grasses, and so on. This is of enormous help when you come to the eventual sorting out, and looking for the special flowers, leaves, etc. needed for the layout and design you have in mind.

The essential thing is to press correctly and firmly. Weight the books very heavily, and leave them undisturbed for at least six to ten weeks in a light, sunny, airy room and one which is quite free from damp. The airing cupboard is not a good place. It is too warm, the very delicate petals will dry out too quickly, and so hard that when the time comes to take them off their blotting paper they will be so brittle and dry that they will crack and split.

There is one exception to this:

*The Quick Dry Method:* Being impatient to get started on the lovely silver dagger-like leaves of the Echinops and some Raspberry leaves, I took a chance, as the leaves are fairly tough. I therefore ironed them (with the heat mark set at Wool) between blotting paper, and a linen cloth over that, pressing hard for about ten minutes. They were then put quickly into the pressing books to spend one night under a brick in the airing cupboard (the door left open). They were dry enough to be used next day in a design. This quick drying was a great asset,

A solid and complicated flower like the trumpet Daffodil must be dissected before being pressed. These photographs show how the flower is cut from its stalk, and carefully divided into two with scissors; then the trumpet and the corolla are separated; and how the pages of the pressing book are rolled closed over the Daffodil sections, so that they will remain in position. Note the label.

instead of the more usual six to ten weeks. I would *not* recommend this method for every flower or leaf, but occasionally a creased petal of say a slightly crinkled Anthemis or Pansy can be saved this way, and encouraged very gently to regain its smoothness by the ironing treatment. But too hot an iron and the bloom or leaf will turn brown, so beware!

*Extra Pressing:* I have used for pressing hard woody stems, like Mimosa or entire Prunus twigs, an old trouser press. Mimosa needs a very heavy weight, or a hard turn on the press. The press can be stood upright, an added advantage when one is short of space!

In the illustration on page 54 can be seen a little home-made flower press. It is not essential, but useful for giving extra pressure to those flowers like Anthemis which have a lumpy corolla. Just three days in between these hard boards, and they can then be quickly transferred into the books. Ask your local handy-man, there's always one around IF you look and enquire hard and often enough, who will be able to make you one.

One Anthemis daisy, with the whiskers of a dismantled Barley head peeping out between the yellow petals.

## ARRANGING THE DESIGN

If it helps you, and you know exactly what flowers you have in your books, draw a design out first, in rough, on PAPER—(*not* on the mounting board). Personally, I prefer to arrange the flowers and stalks on the mounting board and work out the design as I go along. This board is cream on one side and white on the other, and can be obtained from any good art shop. Use the cream side.

Arrange your flowers and stalks on the mounting board. Decide where your centre focal point is to be. Maybe it is the biggest flower, Clematis Nelly Moser, or Clematis President (which is blue, but dries out a rich brown with a stripe down the middle like Nelly Moser).

Place it at the centre near base, leaving enough room for a much smaller, neat little composition of a base design (as shown on page 57) to finish off the picture.

Curves in a design make a picture restful to the eye. Make your curves radiate out from a central base, or from one side like a spray or fan. Give your picture a "swinging" effect, either upwards or downwards.

48

A very light touching-up with poster paint is allowed for white florets and leaves.

The Montana stalk is the one I use for the main dominant line. See that it curves and winds its way up or horizontally, making joins by cutting out pieces of the much needed curve, twist or bend, taken perhaps from another piece of stalk and neatly joining it to the other. Hide the join if necessary with a leaf.

Move the now dry flower-heads, leaves, etc., about the board with a paint brush; as the petals are very fragile, handle them as little as possible.

In my early stages of making flower pictures I wasted four valuable, painstaking hours of arranging (before the flowers were stuck down with the fixative rubberised solution, Copydex), for, when I stood back from the board and sighed a large sigh of relief and satisfaction—oh dear! my sigh blew all the flowers askew and most fell off the board on to the floor! See therefore, that the design is arranged in a quiet, undisturbed room. No sighs! No coughs! No unexpected sneezes—or worse—slamming doors!

Since my early work on making Pressed Flower Pictures, I now find

One white lawn Daisy and Senecio Laxifolius leaves: the dark side of these leaves resembles a Daisy leaf. The common lawn Daisy leaf does not keep its dark green, as does the Senecio.

A flower vase mat suitable for beginners, five inches square, made of lawn Daisies arranged on a dark blue background. The design is not disturbed if you lift and arrange the flowers with a paint brush.

To fix the Daisies in place, turn the brush round, and with the wooden end put a little blob of Copydex on the background, or, if you prefer it, on the back of the flower.

A table mat of Japanese Maple, also suitable for a beginner. Use the same method to lift the delicate leaves, and apply the Copydex with the reversed brush. In the foreground is a dab of Copydex on a tile, ready to hand.

Marking out the size of backing material (tweed) for a seven-inch-square table mat; and cutting carefully along the markings.

Binding the edges together with Sellotape X. Put the mat at the edge of the table, as shown.

Trimming the edges. This mat was made with yellow Anthemis and Cow Parsley; it has a black background.

A home-made press for Anthemis flowers, made by Stanley Hobbs. It is not essential, but very useful for such hard Daisy centres. The mat designs show Honeysuckle, Daffodil (half only!), Delphinium florets, Lady's Bedstraw, Anthemis, two Ash leaves, Woodruff, and Barley whiskers.

it easier to kneel on a rubber cushion and work on the design on the floor. The pressing books on the floor are now all near at hand within arm's length, and one doesn't have the exhausting up-and-down search from a table to floor to find the flower one needs.

Keep the room warm. If by November any of the blotting paper in the books feels damp, just before you remove the flowers off for the design, place the blotting paper (and flowers) on a radiator or in the airing cupboard for a very few minutes. It is very important to see that the flowers, etc., are not damp at all before they are finally sealed into the picture and the picture backed with hardboard.

I never allow, if possible, the flower petals, stalks or leaves to touch one another. As Ruth Webb says in a Victorian Valentine book about one of the artist's designs, when smothered and overdone, "They are all of themselves—too much". Do not clutter up designs. Every stalk, petal and leaf must be shown to its best advantage.

*Equipment*
The outlay is quite small. *Blotting paper* is one of the biggest needs,

54

get a quire at a time. Use *old books* for the pressing. A *paint brush*, use the fluffy end for moving the flowers about, and then turn the brush round, and use the tip of the handle for dipping into the small blob of Copydex. Copydex is an ideal fixative because if you make a mistake you can easily rub it off completely (with a CLEAN finger) and it leaves no mark.

*Scissors* will be needed, but mostly one can snap off the too long stalks with one's nails. To be honest, I find the best tools of all are the nail of my first finger and thumb of the left hand. The right hand holds the brush to move the petals about, and I just assist the brush when I lift a flower from the book to the board.

●place Copydex here for all the daisy type flowers

*Sticking, backgrounds*

When the design is complete, start sticking the flowers, leaves and stalks on to the mounting board. Use the handle of your paint brush, and put a very very little Copydex on the corolla or thickest part of the flower, and just stroke the stalks gently and sparingly with the adhesive.

As you are arranging the design on the *cream* side of the board, and to the required size and shape; and sorting through the labelled pages for suitable shapes and colours, lifting and moving the petals about; it may take hours, or weeks, before you are satisfied with the design and balance, so the petals and leaves you have chosen must be kept as dry as possible in the interval between designing, sticking and framing.

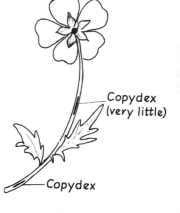

● place Copydex at the back of the buttercup flower

Copydex (very little)

Copydex

Therefore, place very carefully large sheets of blotting paper over the flowers, and then a sheet of glass (previously cut for the frame by any glazier, or ironmongers). See that the glass is free of dust and smears. Then place a blanket over all this, and a brick or two on the top (to continue the pressing). This is only if you have been called away, or there is a long interruption of say two or three days before you can take the finished picture to be framed.

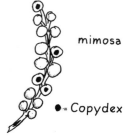

mimosa

● = Copydex

The room must be warm and dry as you work, for if damp is allowed to get in it will eventually spoil the flowers; so this intermediate method is essential before the picture is finally backed with hardboard by the picture framer. Ask him to back it with hardboard, *not* just cardboard.

If, however, you wish to make a picture with a black background (as shown in plates 5 and 8), only a thin piece of cardboard is required

rose petal
delphinium etc

Copydex here only

(reverse side)
clematis, Nelly Moser

— Copydex here only

honeysuckle

Copydex here —
use sparingly

instead of the mounting board, and then buy a piece of black paper at a stationers. (They have all colours.) Gripfix it down on to the cardboard, and see it is smooth and has no wrinkles. White, yellow and cream flowers and grey leaves show up well on black.

*Picture Framing*

Framing your Pressed Flower Picture can be most costly, though on the other hand a simple plain wood is less expensive than, for instance, the painted frames with the attractive gold line.

But, with a little hunting around, a big economy can be made in the use of an old discarded frame which can be found for a few shillings in a junk shop. But beware of woodworm! If it is wormy, treat it first, fill in the worm holes with plastic wood (obtainable in small tins in a hardware shop), then sandpaper over the old frame and regild with gold paint, after an undercoat of size; or after the undercoat finish off with a cream or white paint. *Do not mount the pictures*, otherwise the flowers will not come in direct contact with the glass to remain completely pressed.

Most of my pictures are about 35″ × 32″ but there is a nice oblong size about 13″ × 31″, and this can hang either over a mantelpiece horizontally, or in a narrow wall niche perpendicularly. Another useful size is the one in plate 14, 14″ × 18″.

I get the mounting board cut to exact size needed at a picture framing shop, and order the frame and glass at the same time. The glass and mounting board I return straight home with, for the glass is very important to have as one must use it to keep the flowers free (in the designing stage) from curling up, or absorbing any damp while in the middle of the designing process and before it is finished. To carry the picture down to be firmly backed by hardboard at the shop, I put in temporary picture tacks and Sellotape the glass and board round to ensure no damp is absorbed on the way to the shop. Take too, the precaution of wrapping the picture in a blanket to prevent damp or injury to the edges of the frame when transporting it to the picture framers, and tie it with thick, strong string.

I have been fortunate in finding a framer who is both careful and quick. Speed is so important, as you do not want an unsealed picture to remain in a damp workshop for long, especially when you have, until then, taken such care to keep the flowers dry and firmly pressed.

The hardboard backing to the picture is essential.

*Picture. Design*

You must depend on the stalks for "line", curving upwards, sideways or in a downwards curve to lead the eye to an interesting focal point, and flowing out from this point. The design must be curving, and restful to the eye. It may sometimes be necessary to use the stem only of a nicely curved Primrose stalk and substitute the flower from a more rigid stalk to get the very specially desired curves. The design can radiate out like a fan, from either the side or centre base of the picture.

Four basic designs.

For example, place a large bold Clematis, either Nelly Moser or President, at the centre base of the picture, with one continuous but curving Montana bind going up the middle, to lead the eye up the design. You may have to cut the "twiggle" stalk of the Montana in several places to get the line in one long undulating curve. (See plate 6.) Several of these 30″ by 12″ pictures have at least three or four joins in this perpendicular curved line. The joins are carefully and cunningly hidden, sometimes by a leaf. "Line" to me is like a row of chorus girls. However pretty their faces, without the stalk, or legs in the case of the chorus of dancing girls, and the arms and legs curving to a distinct LINE, the dancing would be nothing. So it is with the flowers in the picture, which depends on the stalk for its line.

The picture looks more "finished off" (if the arrangement is an oval one, or a square), if the very centre base edges are given a compact little

57

design of their own. Neat and tidy. Examples are shown in plates 6 and 8.

The picture in plate 3 is designed to hang either upright or horizontal. Keep the smaller flowers near the top of the picture, or round the edges. Nipplewort is a good "filler-in" of gaping empty spaces or edges in a design, and also Cow Parsley, if on a black background.

**Nipplewort (Compositae family). Grows everywhere on waste ground, and flowers from July to September. Knock the seeds out before pressing. This is a most dainty "filler-in", and one of my favourite dead-heads.**

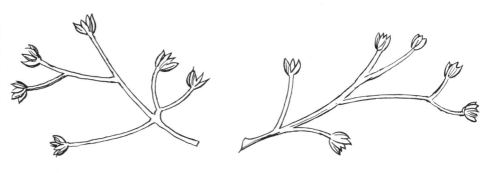

**Placed on a black background, Daffodils (cut in half) make a nice centre base.**

**Very young Honesty seed pods.**

Suitable centre bases to finish off a picture where the focal point is at the centre base: two Ash leaves. There are always two identical leaves at the top of a twig in April or May. These dry out black.

Two Vetch leaves.

Senecio laxifolius leaves, placed upside down and right side up alternately, make a pattern of dark grey and white.

59

*The use of Butterflies, and where to obtain them*

To give a picture a more natural look add a butterfly or two if there is room. They transform a picture into a lighter, daintier design and somehow give it "life". Butterflies can be ordered or chosen from The World Wide Butterfly shop in the intriguing Lanes of Brighton in Sussex. Here you can choose to your heart's desire those colours which will best suit the tone of your picture.

Otherwise, you can be lucky in finding an old case of butterflies in a sale. Old junk shops are happy hunting grounds, not only for old picture frames; and a case of butterflies from an entomologist's old collection can often be bought for a small sum. But the older the butterfly, the more you must beware that the mounting-pin in the centre of the body is not rusted in too firmly. If it is, put the butterfly on a piece of damp flannel in a warm place in a box for about an hour or so. You will then find the wings have become movable, and the pin should also come out without too much trouble. The pliable wings may then be moved into any position you wish. Placed in a dry atmosphere again, the wings will remain firm and set. Some of the butterflies in these pictures were bred by a young amateur entomologist, Peter Hawkey of Sevenoaks in Kent.

May I here assure my readers that these butterflies were allowed to breed, and were not wantonly destroyed. Peter supplies other amateur collectors; and some of the butterflies he breeds to let go in the Weald of Kent to multiply, and enhance the countryside.

Peter selected special brown and orange and yellow and cream specimens for me to blend in with the dried pressed flowers. Bright red or blue butterflies would be out of place on these beige-chrome designs and distract the eye.

The cabbage white butterflies were supplied by an ardent gardener in a Sussex village, who was only too glad to give a few of the many hundreds which were laying eggs on his cabbages. The white butterflies, both open, as in flight, or "resting", look lovely in a picture on a black background.

Do see you handle these butterflies gently, and do not knock off their antennae. If you do—go to the broom cupboard, and replace the antennae with two curvy broom bristles! Put a tiny bit of Copydex on at the end of each bristle and gently insert it under the butterfly's head. As the butterfly's body easily disintegrates, give it a false body cut out from, say, a cancelled brown postage stamp. I especially mention a cancelled brown stamp because of the small black lines which run across the brown! If you cut a small shape (a) out of the stamp it makes a good substitute for a body, being of the same burnt umber colour. Or you can cut out a "body" this shape (b) and paint it and shade it, or, if you have any old magazine or old unwanted books on butterflies, cut out the paper butterfly's body and substitute it for the real butterfly.

To fix the butterfly, hold it very gently, but press firmly on its brittle body, when it will become slightly flatter. Then very carefully put a little Copydex down the centre of its body or, if you prefer, put the blob of Copydex on the mounting board itself, on a flower or wherever you want it to be. Place the butterfly at an angle. Never straight.

# 4

## *For Beginners*

T RY A SIMPLE table-mat to start with.

*Table Mats*

The Red Japanese Maple leaf shows up well on a yellow or chrome background; or the yellow Anthemis daisies (the Anthemis needs very heavy pressing) and a few grey Cinerarea Diamond leaves (white side uppermost) on a pale blue or black background. Or one Nelly Moser Clematis with dark, almost black Montana leaves, on a white background. You will need:

Pieces of glass or perspex cut to say sizes 7″ × 7″, 6″ × 6″ or 5″ × 5″. The 5″ × 5″ are suitable for a glass or vase mat.
Coloured paper bought in a stationer's shop, or coloured blotting paper.
Copydex.
Cardboard (thick).
Sellotape, X, of any colour.
Felt for backing, or a piece of thick tweed material from an old skirt.

An ironmonger or glazier will cut the glass, which can be of either 24 oz. or 32 oz. thickness, and costs only about 9d. for each size mentioned above.

Cut the coloured paper to the preferred size, and stick it on to the thick cardboard, and stick the cardboard on to the felt; or use an odd piece of tweed as backing.

Choose your flowers and lay out your design. Let the edges of the petals and leaves stand out, and see that the edges of the petals do not touch each other, and remember always that the stalks help to guide the eye along the flowing line of the design, whether a circular design or upright. Stick the flowers and leaves down and place the glass on.

Bind the edges together with one of the colours of Sellotape X. This

In autumn the star-shaped leaves of Japanese Maple cover the grass, like sparks, or burning embers. I gather as many as I can into an outspread handkerchief or head scarf, so that they may be carried home without damage, where these glorious leaves will immediately be pressed. Here you see the leaves after four weeks of firm pressing in their blotting paper bed, under the weight of two bricks. They are arranged under glass for a table mat design. Anthemis flowers are rather huddled in the centre, as if to escape the flames of the crimson Maple leaves, and Senecio leaves are arranged round to resemble smoke, and soften the edges.

operation is more easily carried out if you place the mat just over the edge of a table.

For a very simple design, shown overleaf is a 5″ × 5″ table mat for a vase made of Herb Robert (or Wild Geranium) leaves. Pick these towards late summer when they have had a chance to turn to this delightful dark crimson and look almost like lace.

Try the little lawn Daisy, this needs only about four weeks' pressing, on a blue or black background. Notice some Daisies have pretty pink edges, especially where the cultivated Bachelor Button has been growing. The bees do the rest! Shown here is a table mat designed on a black background. Mimosa, and the Limnanthese (or Poached Egg plant) which keep their colour well; Clovers, Buttercups, and the little lawn Daisy, and the edges of the design softened with various grasses.

Make a set of dinner mats with Hydrangea florets as I did. Each floret should be separately dried and then reassembled into one large flower, keeping the darker petals for the base of the circle to give "roundness". They keep their intriguing green-blue and crimson for about three years.

When sticking the Anthemis daisy only put Copydex on the back

63

A table mat design made of Japanese Maple leaves: several of the leaves were dismantled, and arranged to form a pattern.

A flower vase mat, five inches square, with a design of Herb Robert leaves. A suggested first step for a beginner.

The table mat with lawn Daisies on a blue background seen in the making on page 50. It is no good standing Daisies aside in a jam jar of water to wait until you are ready. Unless placed in full sun, they will close their petals. All these Daisies had their petals touched up with white poster paint. Senecio at corners.

Limnanthese flowers against a black background make a pretty table mat.

of the corolla, NOT on the petals, it is not necessary, as the glass keeps them flat and in place.

*Door Finger Plates*

Door finger plates are also very easily and cheaply made from Polyglaze or the ready-made transparent perspex: or, ready-made transparent finger plates can be bought in a hardware shop.

You will need:

A piece of card.

2 screws to affix, top and bottom.

Cut a piece of ordinary card about 12″ × 3″ or 11″ × 2¾″ and stick on your flowers and stalks. In a door finger plate the stalks are the most important thing of all, for you are working on a very confined, limited space, and the eye must be guided upwards; and the best means for this are curved stalks. Make an interesting centre base, e.g. two identical Vetch leaves, or Ivy leaves, a single Daisy or two very small black Ash leaves.

A "mock" Periwinkle can be made from five or six Delphinium petals, with incorporated stamens from a cast-out imperfect-petalled flower of a Welsh Poppy. Use the loose petals of Anthemis daisy, fix them with Copydex to the bud of a buttercup.

Grasses are essential in a door finger plate's limited space as their stalks guide the eye. Bright colours are not important.

Over the design place the perspex or Polyglaze. This is pliable and can be cut at home, with scissors. Lay it on the design and bind the edges to the cardboard with the transparent Sellotape very tightly. A centre screw either end is all that is needed to fix it to the door.

Look at plate 23c. In this design there is no colour except beiges and browns, but it still pleases the eye, it is so uncluttered and simple, and the stems balance the picture.

I picked the Clover in a car park in Polperro in June, where I had my lunch and where sharp eyes and eager fingers were ever at the ready, for possible "pressers"! All went into the little jam jar of water to keep them fresh, brought along balanced in a basin to avoid slopping of water when descending the steep Cornish lanes!

Mrs. Ginger's first door finger plate design, made as a beginner.

The Wild Barley was found in a deserted old Vicarage backyard, in what was once the Vicar's hen-run. This Wild Barley is a "creeper". I pick it to pieces, and as this door finger plate was designed in bed I found it had a most irritating way of clinging on to either the sheets and blankets or worse—my brushed nylon nightie. And I was awakened sharply at 2 a.m. to find a Barley sneaking its way up my sleeve—very tickley and very spikey!

At the base centre of the door finger plate is a single leaf of the Herb Robert. Seed heads of deep brown from a pond grass gives the picture "body", and Nipplewort, with its seeds lightly shaken out before pressing, take the eye to the top of the design also.

Buttercups and Honeysuckle make an attractive motif, or five Delphinium petals arranged to look like a Periwinkle flower, with the stamens of the little yellow Welsh Poppy, grasses, and the florets of Ground Elder to fill in the narrow space of the door finger plates.

*Trays*

Hardboard for backing, painted first with a sealer, and then two coats of Japlac, or another lacquer paint. A picture framer will frame the tray in ordinary simple picture-framing wood, and you can screw the handles on later if required.

*Pictures by a beginner*

After my talk on B.B.C. "Woman's Hour" Mrs. Ginger was one listener inspired enough to enquire for more details on pressing flowers. We did in fact develop a kind of correspondence course, and answers and questions travelled with lightning speed between us! She sent me parcels of plants and even seeds (of a red Broom) which are now duly growing in a little pot in my "green-house", the airing cupboard. Within a few days all the seeds had germinated and within a few weeks were able to be pricked out. One day Mrs. J.G. sent me a parcel containing two enormous blue Artichoke Thistle heads—with one cheeky note saying, "I dare you to press these"! And since this book has got into print, I am sure I owe it partly to one of her letters which in June contained three four-leafed clovers! For luck! She also sent me a magazine, the pages filled with pressed Whitebeam leaves,

Another finger plate design by Mrs. Ginger.

66

after I had bewailed the scarcity of this tree in Kent, for it likes chalk, and grows well in Surrey. By October a parcel arrived containing her first effort at making a Pressed Flower Picture. A great accomplishment indeed, and I gave it what I hope was kind, constructive and encouraging criticism, and I added tips and advice for her future efforts—for it does take effort; and as she so rightly said, it is the getting it framed which takes the time; but is the completion of months of patience and perhaps mistakes, but by mistakes one learns!

This attractive little picture was the first composed of flowers pressed and collected by Mrs. Joy Ginger. Although it is her first attempt it has the overall tone and arrangement of a person who is not new to the subject of pressing flowers. But in fact it is a beginner's work. This picture was accomplished soon after hearing my talk on "Woman's Hour" and reading my published articles in magazines. The rest of

Mrs. Ginger's first picture.

her very exceptional talent has been added to my experience and advice.

A very successful combination it has proved to be. One can always learn by one's own mistakes and misuse of certain leaves and colours, and this knowledge can only come by years of experiment; and I have learnt a lot through Mrs. Ginger's numerous questions about the snags one is liable to meet.

For example, overcrowding (which she has just managed to avoid!) because one is very tempted to fill one's first picture with all the flowers and leaves one has picked and pressed that summer! One must NOT do this! Hold back! To help overcome this try doing two or even three pictures at a time.

Her use of the red Saxifrage is very pretty and the lovely star-like dominance of the white Hattie's Pincushion flower (Astrantia) and the giant Spiraea's golden plumes which give the picture length. The various green leaves will alas, in time, turn brown, but the dark young Sycamore leaves are a very good choice and will remain, or even darken in colour. Likewise the little Woodruff leaves and flowers, they darken too as they dry off. Woodruff is very similar to Lady's Bedstraw, both very dainty "fillers in" for softening edges. The mauve Pansy would be better exchanged for a yellow and black one, for these last longer than the mauve.

Her second picture is a little over-cluttered and spoilt by too many dismantled Barley whiskers! Two at the left-hand side base (7 o'clock) would have been sufficient. The dominance of the dark Montana leaves and varying types of leaves give the design "body", and there is a lot to look at. The Rose petals (Iceberg) have, one can see, been very well pressed, only a few to a page in the drying book. Pressing too many together in a page only results in a spotting mildew but these are perfect. The Delphinium, made up of only six large petals instead of its more usual number of sixteen, has a superimposed centre of several Delphinium "middles". A cunning move this and very effective!

Picture No. 3 is a "winner"! But it would have been better to place the two top Poppy buds and stems lower down and so give more width at the base, so leaving the Honeysuckle to do the final domination at the top.

One step forward! Mrs. Ginger's second picture, a more advanced effort.

Another charming picture by Mrs. Joy Ginger.

Again she has made subtle use of the Hattie's Pincushion flower (Astrantia) and placed it as the Rose's centre. The dainty little blue Forget-me-not-type flowers, alas, will not retain their blue. It would have been better to dismantle the pale yellow florets of say Yarrow, and put these instead. Yellows keep their colour best.

Two door finger plates (pages 65 and 66) are also most attractive as samples of Mrs. Ginger's work. A lovely "line" guides the eye upwards made with the stem of Montana, and though the leaves are of an interesting shape they have been picked green and will therefore turn a beigey-brown in a year's time. Likewise the white petals of white Campion on the black background design. If one does use white, choose only the lawn Daisy. The Cow Parsley will need touching up with a very little white poster paint.

69

*The important rules are:*

NOT to look at your flowers pressing in blotting paper until at least 6 to 10 weeks.

Keep the room dry and airy.

Use very little adhesive for sticking the flowers, leaves, etc., down; and avoid flowers which have complicated corollas.

This is a most absorbing and happy pastime and can indeed be called a Collage of Flowers in our present Elizabethan Age, as the Victorians did in the 1840s, making their pictures of anything from feathers, shells, seaweed, strands of hair, and sand.

Go out, you "Flower Power" people, and have fun!

# 5

## *Far Away Flowers*

L ISTED HERE ARE plants which would be ideal for making Pressed
Flower Pictures, but which I have not been able to secure; for instance,
if I had wherewithal to visit these lovely countries, namely Australia,
New Zealand, Greece and the Prairies in America, many flowers
would surely reach the pressing books! I must emphasise, however,
that the particular flowers I mention are, as yet, UN-tested for suitability by me, but because some belong to the reasonably safe varieties,
*legiminosae* (Vetch and Trefoil family) ranunculus (Buttercup) I
advise you to have a go! One flower which catches the eye in Australia
is the Flannel Flower *(Actinotus helianthi)*. It has a petal texture
similar to the Edelweiss and blooms profusely in spring and summer.
Being white, to a soft grey-green, it would show up well with added
grey foliage on a black background. The Pink Flannel Flower grows
in New South Wales and in the Blue Mountains. This variety flowers
in January and February.

Likewise, if only it was within an afternoon's walk away, and not a
few thousand miles, I would "beg, borrow and steal" the delightfully
vivid little gentian-type flower of the tiny shrub *Leschenaultia biloba*.
Its intense blue is on a par with that of the Gentian Verna, and though
I have not myself tested the Gentian flower (from Scotland or Switzer-
land) for colour retention, I know Gentians are used widely in Switzer-
land for little dried posy flower picture arrangements.

As yellow-petalled flowers are a fairly safe bet for colour retention
(up to three years or so) try the small St. John's Wort *(Hypericum
gramineum)*. It flowers in summer and resembles a cross between a
Buttercup and a Flax, and tends to "take over" the land from the
Australian farmers! Another flower which looks inviting is the Flat Pea
*(Platylobium formosum)*. Press the flowers only. These are yellow with

71

a touch of red at the back of the standard petal and on the "wings". It flowers in spring in the sandy parts of Queensland, New South Wales, Victoria and Tasmania. It is a little like the Broom family.

Other flowers which might become eventual "pressers" are the Parrot Pea, yellow and red, and the Toothed Guinea flower which is yellow. The Geraldton wax plant looks dainty and inviting enough to be pressed with its pink petals, like those of the Saxifrage. It is common on the limestone hills of Western Australia and flowers in early spring and throughout the summer. I like its delicate, dainty stem and foliage, always a point to look for. Any of the yellows in the ranunculus family are possible pressers, and though they retain their colour for not more than three or four years, allow for this, place them on a black background, and allow this background to enhance the later paling of the petals' colour.

It would be nice to try the yellow woolly Everlasting Flower (*Helichrysum semi papposum*) which we in England must buy from a seedsman, but which abounds in great carpets of this golden flower in spring in Western Australia and in Tasmania, it grows high up in rich sandy loams in late spring. It would need a hard, heavy pressing, at least three bricks for three weeks, then easing off to allow a little air to circulate within the pages to avoid mildew.

New Zealand has a profusion of flowers too, especially those of the *ranunculaceae* family, and also has the leaf to offer us from the Senecio plant which I often use in my pictures.

Another country noted for its beautiful flowers is Greece, and has one which I have no hesitation in recommending, the Delphinium, which grows wild on the Island of Lesbos.

Now come with me on the magic carpet to see the wealth of flowers which grow on the American Prairies. Again the list is endless, but I leave the decision to you as regards choice, and to experiment, as I had to, for retention of colour and "line" suitability.

Bedstraw, Yellow Parsley, Buttercups throng the meadows and hill slopes. Marsh Marigolds brighten the swampier places, and I was intrigued to see that the buds of this flower are sometimes used as a substitute for the French Capers used in cooking.

Blue Larkspur grows here too; the Prairies are a botanist's paradise!

Golden Rods and their many ancestors, Sunflower (use the petals only, and then reassemble), Black-eyed Susan, Coreopsis, the Jewel-weed, which is like a Mimulus and is to be found in damp ground. Pick the flower only. Try Loosestrife, belonging to the Primrose family but a brighter yellow.

The Fringed Puccoon attracts me, with its yellow trumpet-like flower, to be found on the Prairies, Manitoba and west to Texas and British Columbia in April and July. The flower is long and tube-like, with frilly-edged petals. It resembles in shape the Tobacco flower, and any flower with an unusual shape and an uncomplicated "middle" is worth pressing.

Tick Trefoils, Vetches, White Clover; all are found in the Prairies. Butter and Eggs, a two-toned cream and orange flower, like a miniature Snapdragon, is similar to our English Toadflax.

All the many Vetches are attractive, and even if their colour does not last very long, their twisting turning stems and pretty leaves help many a stiff design to loosen up: for example, the purple Milk Vetch, like the tufted Vetch.

The Partridge Pea has yellow rounded petals with an eye-catching purple dark centre. It grows in sunny, sandy fields. Once, while watching an exciting, noisy, gun-shooting film of Texans, my companion enjoyed the story while I had to confess that all I had really enjoyed and was interested in between the noisy gunfire and galloping horses was when I spied some lovely wafting grasses, blowing in a light breeze against a blue blue sky! The grasses were swaying in the very corner, just within camera range! It gave me more of a thrill to see them than the daring Texas Rangers!

"Ideal for pressing," I murmured to my companion through a haze of smoke and peppermints!

Readers in the countries I have mentioned and elsewhere in the world will have the fun, with, I hope, the help of my experience which I have set down in this book, to find out for themselves—and what could be more enjoyable than that?

73

# INDEX

*Black and white illustrations are indexed in italic figures; colour plates in bold figures*

77

# THE
# COLOUR
# PLATES

**PLATE 1**  25″ × 34″. This was my first picture. I had not learnt to keep
the number of flowers, leaves, etc., down to the minimum,
but I was getting the idea of a swinging downwards or
upwards by the use of stalks. Nor had I realised the
importance of not allowing a petal or leaf to touch another.
The fronds of the Hard Fern (Barren) show up well
at the lower left and right of the picture. The floret
of Marigold, without its petals, makes a centre for the
Rose petals.

**PLATE 2**      24″ × 35″. This picture (my fifth) shows the first steps towards simplifying a design, and keeping out the many flowers which have been pressed, and which I was tempted to include: you must be firm! The butterfly has a train of Goose Grass.

**PLATE 3**    32″ × 24″. This large picture has been designed to hang upright or horizontally. The tones are beige ('Peace' petals) blue-grey (the leaves of the Globe flower, Echinops) and darker blue (the Jackmanii Clematis). The under side of this Clematis flower is a paler grey-blue. To break up the pointed, dagger-like line of the Globe thistle leaves are the leaves of Cineraria Maritima Diamond (see left base). The three circular flowers are made of rose petals, 'Peace' for the large one, and the white floribunda 'Iceberg' for the smaller ones: these dry out to a cream, and placing the darker petals at the base of the circle gives an effect of shading. This is a point not to be missed, as the arrangement gives a rounded effect.

I was impatient to get started on these lovely pointed silver leaves, so I took a chance to use the quick-dry pressing method, and ironed them (with the heat-mark set at Wool).

**PLATE 4** 25" × 34½". A large picture of mixed flowers and leaves. A little too crammed with flowers: but to maintain some semblance of design, the stalks radiate out all round towards the edges. The three Delphiniums give height. As the Rose petals are still pink, an Anthemis flower is placed on them; its yellow will blend in well when the Rose petals start to turn brown.

Pamela McDowall 1967

**PLATE 5**  13″ × 17″. A black background. The design is made entirely of the silvery grey undersides of leaves, with the exception of six Senecio leaves, three of which are placed on three dark Honeysuckle leaves; and these are placed on Raspberry leaves; this helps to break up the predominantly grey tones. Two Echinops leaves lead off (at 2 o'clock and 8 o'clock) with their spear-like points. The grey flower buds belong to the Senecio shrub, and are not, as you might think, Raspberry buds. The roundness of Clover is needed as a contrast to the pointed leaves. Below the Clovers is a Cineraria Diamond leaf. Two lawn Daisies fill in a little gap, and there is one yellow Anthemis daisy, nestling in with three white Anthemis Montana flowers, and it is on these white petals that a little cheating is advised. Paint each petal with white poster paint, and allow this to dry for a few minutes before sticking the petal on to the design. It will not require added pressing, if the painting is done with a few quick strokes with a not-too-wet brush. Also used is the underside of the silver Aspen leaf.

**PLATE 6**    24″ × 32″. Again Montana stalks take the lead, but the large Clematis President dominates the picture. To balance the design, Clematis Nelly Moser and the beige of the Iceberg Rose petals are interspersed among Mimosa, Buttercups, Honeysuckle, Anthemis, and Primula. The Honeysuckle twine (from a variety which has a green and yellow spotted leaf, and no flower) helps to give a curvy, restful look. I have used the Earth Nut leaf (at left, 10 o'clock) and Montana leaves, very dark brown. Laburnum and Mimosa round off the centre base

Pamela McDowall 1967

**PLATE 7**    15″ × 18½″. The colour motif in this picture is made up of orange Welsh Poppies, yellow Buttercups and Anthemis daisies, and made-up yellow daisies from loose, odd petals of the Anthemis. I used a Buttercup bud and stalk to 'collage' these made-up daisies, resting the yellow petals on the dark brown leaves of the Cherry Prunus. Very small pink fern leaves complete this spray design.

Pamela McDowall 1968

**PLATE 8**    14″ × 18″. Cow Parsley, Honeysuckle, Anthemis, Buttercups, Clover, Daisy, Vetch (yellow), Celandine, Limnanthese, Primrose, Mouse Tail grass, Senecio (the grey
leaves at the base); against a black background.

**PLATE 9a**   13″ × 30″. A blue and grey mixture, Delphiniums, Honeysuckle, two little lawn Daisies in centre base, with a touch of Bachelor's Button's pink-edged petals. Clematis Montana twine is used for the Delphinium stalk. Clover. The various grey leaves are the Senecio (at the base), Cineraria Diamond, and Echinops.

**PLATE 9b**   13″ × 30″. A predominantly blue-toned picture, composed of Delphinium petals, the flowers in their entirety, and buds, Clematis Jackmanii, with their petals wrong side up, to give a lighter tone of blue-grey; Mimosa's yellow breaks up the blue, and I have added six Mimosa leaves to give a helping upward swing to the design. Honeysuckle peeps out at centre base, and fills in the larger gaps. Note the dark Honeysuckle leaves slanting in the opposite way to the superimposed-type of Delphinium left of the picture. The butterflies seem to find their own way around! There is one Montana leaf at the right-hand base.

**PLATE 10**     $25\frac{1}{2}"\times34\frac{1}{2}"$. This large design turned into the shape of a swan! I felt tempted to put a pointed leaf at the end of its 'head' for a beak; instead I placed a humble lawn Daisy. The Clematis is Madame Edward André, a red which dries out a maroon colour, like the Blackberry and Prunus leaves next to it. Mimosa lies on these leaves to show them off to their best advantage. Note the one Celandine, once yellow, now white. Branching out on either side is Privet.

**PLATE 11a**     13″ × 20″. Tones: varying-coloured browns, creams, orange, yellow. A Montana stalk goes winding up the centre line, joined with a twig of Cherry Prunus and its leaves. Mimosa is placed on Prunus leaves to give it a good dark background. Clematis Nelly Moser, with a butterfly on each set at an angle; Honeysuckle, Nipple-wort, and Sutton's Sunshine Flower. Also, two flowers only of Montbretia.

**PLATE 11b**     13″ × 30″. A most satisfying size to work on. Several joins have been made, to get the Montana stalk to curve at just the right places. It is a soft, grey-toned design, with Echinops leaves dried by the quick-dry method. Sparking outward from the Montana stem are Clovers, and two Astrantia, or Hattie's Pincushion: pink, star-shaped flowers. The Pond grass (dark brown) was a gift from my goldfish! The Honeysuckle is the Lonicera Halleand variety, reassembled to be like the common hedgerow variety.

My favourite design.

**PLATE 12**     $34'' \times 25\frac{1}{2}''$. In early spring I had an idea for an autumn picture, so the following leaves were collected in spring: Maple, Chestnut, Aspen, Poplar, and Oak; and pressed when the leaves were very tender, and had an almost translucent appearance of greeny-yellow and pink. The other leaves were reds and golds, the true colours of autumn, and were picked up on my way home from shopping, the leaves placed with loving care on the groceries or in my pocket handkerchief. These were put into the pressing books while the lunch was cooking. In the picture, the leaves seem caught in the swirl of an autumn breeze; and the guiding lines for this effect come from a few very thin twigs of the Cherry Prunus.

Parks and pavements and grass verges provide town dwellers with all they need for leafy designs. Do not despise the interesting shape of a folded or bent leaf; it makes for a more natural look of leaves in a sudden upward flurry of wind. Note the silver aspen leaf placed on a darker leaf to show up its outline.

**PLATE 13**  17″ × 20″. The tones of this black-background picture are yellow, cream, white and grey. The flowers and leaves came from as far afield as Northumberland and Bridport in Dorset; the Mimosa from a florist, the humble Clover picked in a car park in Polperro in Cornwall. Note the touching-up technique of painting on a very little white poster paint on the Clover, Cow Parsley and Honeysuckle. Note too the curving of the Barren Brome grasses, which give the whole picture an effect of roundness. These grasses, incidentally, were spied by me growing beside the road while I was held up in a traffic jam outside Honiton! The wild Barley whiskers give a frosty, sparkling effect to this spring-like picture.

**PLATE 14**   14″ × 18″. This little 'mixture of all sorts' picture was inspired by the two small Clematis flowers given to me by a sandy-haired artist. The *décor* of his flat is in orange, brown and blue, and this picture is composed of the colours which will be most happy with these wall and carpet tones. The orange Montbretia flower keeps its colour well, and so do the two Anthemis daisies, yellow and a deeper chrome yellow. Note that the petals are backed with Honeysuckle leaves (which turn dark brown if pressed in too warm a temperature) which set the yellow points of the petals off well. Once again it is the line of stalks which gives the picture its design; it would be nothing without them. The Clematis is *florida bicolor*.

Pamela McDowall. 1968

**PLATE 15**  24″ × 34″. This picture has very much the same simplified design as Plate 10, but here I used a strong Nelly Moser flower, and a number of grey leaves grown from seed in the airing cupboard! Cineraria Maritima Diamond and Centaurea Gymnocarpa; barren fronds of the Hard Fern, and Ash leaves. Round the edge of the design is the lacy, delicate little Lady's Bedstraw, and Primula.

**PLATE 16a**  12″ × 30″. Various grasses make up this light, 'airy-fairy' design, helped out by the herbaceous long-lasting Anthemis daisy, Montbretia, and Welsh Poppies. Otherwise the flowers are mostly to be found in the fields and verges, Nipplewort, Clover, Buttercups and Daisies. The base is made up in darker contrast with Raspberry leaves and a Blackberry leaf (centre base), and the Senecio leaf, which is a good substitute for the Daisy leaf. In such a design, avoid overcrowding: and notice that it is the line of the stalks which give the picture balance.

**PLATE 16b**  12″ × 30″. Clematis Montana twine and leaves, Sycamore leaves, Ground Elder flowers, 3 Primroses, 3 Clovers, Honeysuckle, Agapanthus flowers from Ghana.

**PLATE 17**     19″ × 23½″. This picture is for a beginner. You must have caught the early Mimosa in the shops in February. The silver leaves are of Cineraria Diamond, which can be bought as plants in May, or grown from seed, as mine were, in a box; germinated in the airing cupboard, transplanted later into 'roomier lodgings', and kept on my window sill until the warmer weather, when they were big enough to be transplanted. The Mimosa and Buttercup stems give the upward swing, to burst into a mass of little Cow Parsley florets. These and the nine Senecio leaves were touched up with white poster paint with a very dry brush. The two large 'flowers' are circles of the floribunda Iceberg rose petals. These have a nodding acquaintance with three yellow Anthemis daisies, which are such good retainers of colour.

The yellow surround matches the buttercups, but I cannot emphasise enough how important it is NOT to have the picture mounted, as the petals *must* come into contact with the glass when framed.

Pamela McDowall 1968

**PLATE 18**   26″ × 34½″. 'Fireworks': a golden, cream-toned picture. The stalks give the design a swinging effect upwards and downwards. The fluffy-type Mimosa joins in a general swing of Iceland Poppies, Anthemis and Buttercups. Earth Nut leaves have taken the place of the Poppy leaves. The design would be nothing without the dotting about of the Nipplewort. The centre base is made up of Senecio leaves placed alternately grey and green side up. Note the two Vetch leaves in the base, which proved elusive during a week's search of the pressing books! Clover has been incorporated, and Hydrangea florets, green toned, fill in the space, like the Woodruff and two grasses.

**PLATE 19a**     $13\frac{1}{2}'' \times 31''$. Montana stalk is the central curving line, with curves of any conveniently shaped stalks branching outwards to support Honeysuckle. The petals of the Floribunda Rose Iceberg, and umbel florets of the Ground Elder; Pond grass, and one solitary white Clover. The leaves are of the lovely flowering Prunus trees; in autumn the leaves are blown along the street and the pathways, and are retrieved by me on my way back from shopping. Their colours are reddish browns to yellows, vermilions and crimson.

**PLATE 19b**     Honeysuckle, Clematis Montana stem, Frangipani flowers from Ghana, and leaves of Senecio Greyii.

**PLATE 20**   'It's the spaces that count' rings true in this simple design.
A small picture, but just big enough to show off any thin
stems of curving Montana. The centre flower is made up
of Iceberg rose petals, with the stamens of a Welsh poppy
placed in the circle. The grey underside of Raspberry
leaves (which grow wild at the bottom of my garden)
make good mock rose leaves. To balance the Montana
curves are the stems and buds of Montbretia, a neat,
bright and welcome addition to a rather soft-toned
design. Each floret of the Honeysuckle was pressed and
dried separately, and then reassembled as it would normally
grow, buds in the middle, gradually working outwards
to more open florets; and though the Montbretia seems
to be sharing the same stem, it does not matter, so long
as there is a simple, interesting design. The very dark
leaves are taken from a Clematis. They provide a strong,
deep brown contrast to the other paler tones.

There is, however, a glaring mistake in the very centre,
two stalks leading to nowhere! They should have been
snipped off at the very edge of the petals, or placed
underneath. This shows how important it is not to do a
picture in a rush. I shall for ever regret not noticing those
two stalks going nowhere before it was too late, and the
picture was framed and securely backed. This picture
was shown on television in the making, and the general
flurry and whirring of the camera was perhaps the reason
for my mistake.

**PLATE 21a**     11″ × 17″. This is one of my smallest pictures of all. The dark leaves are the result of pruning the Cherry Prunus; tender, dark crimson new leaves, but now dark brown. The two varieties of Anthemis, yellow daisies, look well in the brown tones. Montbretia flowers add a valuable orange colour. Mimosa rests, where possible, on dark leaves. Two Iceland Poppies are placed one on the other to give a deeper colour of melon. The two Mouse Tail grasses (left, 11 o'clock) lead the eye off, and yet my eye is immediately led to the right (5 o'clock) to balance.

**PLATE 21b**     6″ × 6″. Honeysuckle leaves (Halleand variety) really grow in pairs on either side of the stem. The stalk is a Primrose stalk. This butterfly's antennae came from the broom cupboard.

**PLATE 21c**     6″ × 6″. Honeysuckle leaves; the stalk is a well-pressed Anthemis stem. Broom bristles in this butterfly's antennae. He has a 'body' of a franked brown fourpenny stamp—see the little stripes?